WINNIE MANDELA
THE SOUL OF SOUTH AFRICA

WINNIE MANDELA

THE SOUL OF SOUTH AFRICA

BY MILTON MELTZER
Illustrated by Stephen Marchesi

VIKING KESTREL

With special thanks to Monceba Lubanga
M. M.

VIKING KESTREL
Published by the Penguin Group
Viking Penguin Inc., 40 West 23rd Street, New York, New York 10010, U.S.A.
Penguin Books Ltd, 27 Wrights Lane, London W8 5TZ England
Penguin Books Australia Ltd, Ringwood, Victoria, Australia
Penguin Books Canada Ltd, 2801 John Street, Markham, Ontario, Canada L3R 1B4
Penguin Books (N.Z.) Ltd, 182–190 Wairau Road, Auckland 10, New Zealand

Penguin Books Ltd, Registered Offices: Harmondsworth, Middlesex, England

First published in 1986 by Viking Penguin Inc.
Published simultaneously in Canada
Text copyright © Milton Meltzer, 1986
Illustrations copyright © Stephen Marchesi, 1986
All rights reserved

WOMEN OF OUR TIME® is a registered trademark of Viking Penguin Inc.

Library of Congress Cataloging in Publication Data
Meltzer, Milton. Winnie Mandela: the soul of South Africa.
(Women of our time)
Summary: With an emphasis on her early years, covers the life
of Winnie Mandela, who married a prominent fighter for racial equality
in South Africa and later became a leader in her own right.
1. Mandela, Winnie—Juvenile literature.   2. Civil
rights workers—South Africa—Biography—Juvenile
literature.   3. South Africa—Race relations—Juvenile
literature.   [1. Mandela, Winnie.   2. Civil rights
workers.   3. Blacks—Biography.   4. South Africa—Race relations]
I. Marchesi, Stephen, ill.   II. Title.   III. Series.
DT779.955.M36M45   1986   323.4'092'4 [92] 86-5531   ISBN 0-670-81249-8

Printed in the United States of America by Haddon Craftsmen, Bloomsburg, Pennsylvania
Set in Garamond #3
5   7   9   10   8   6   4

CONTENTS

WINNIE MANDELA
THE SOUL OF SOUTH AFRICA

1

I Will Get
My Land Back

On that Saturday afternoon, Winnie Mandela was sitting quietly at home in Soweto, a black township in South Africa. Suddenly there was loud banging on her door. Before she could open it, several policemen with guns pushed their way in. You know you're not allowed to live here, they said. We're taking you to the police station. When she refused to leave, two of the men grabbed her by the arms and dragged her out.

What was her crime? Living in her own home.

Outside her house, hundreds of black neighbors

had gathered, chanting their support. As the police shoved her into a patrol car, she said: "I am charged with a crime that does not exist in most of the democratic civilized world—being at home. This law should not be obeyed by any human being."

Winifred Madikizela was born in Bizana, a rural district in Pondoland, on September 26, 1936. It is mountain country, one of the poorest areas of South Africa, along its eastern side. Her father, Columbus Madikizela, was the principal of a primary school, and her mother, Gertrude, had taught domestic science. Winnie was the fifth of their nine children. Her mother was very religious. She made the children pray aloud many times a day. Winnie often heard her asking God to give her another son. It made Winnie feel she must prove that a girl was worth as much as a boy.

When Winnie was seven, she watched one of her sisters sicken of tuberculosis and die, coughing up blood, while her mother knelt beside the bed, begging God to save her child. After that, Gertrude seemed to shrink to nothingness. She sat in dark corners, praying silently. She died before she was forty, worn out with illness.

Winnie's grief was eased by the big extended family she grew up in. Her home was a group of eight grass-roofed huts where three generations lived. Her father, a tall dignified man, loved his children. His school pay was terribly low, but Columbus Madikizela fed his family well with what he raised in his pastureland and orchard. The children shared in the farmwork before and after school. They all ate their evening meal around huge log fires, listening to tribal tales the old people told. Winnie ran barefoot on the rolling green hills, played ball with the boys, made clay animal toys. It was a happy growing time, so far from the pain and troubles of black life in the cities.

At school Winnie studied English, mathematics, history, the sciences. She got a glimpse of the world beyond Bizana. She learned how huge the continent of Africa is—three times the size of the United States.

If not for her father, Winnie might have grown up with a twisted view of the history of her country. The textbooks were written by whites. They were always saying that a white person had "discovered" this great river or that high mountain in Africa, as though there had been no black people there to see these marvels before a superior person from another continent came upon them.

The history books told a story of the past that tried to justify white rule over the blacks. Winnie's father pointed out the lies, and then told her the truth.

This is the only country in the world, he said, which

by law denies the great majority of the people their rights just because their skin is not white. Think, he said: there are less than five million whites here but twenty-seven million of us . . .

When Winnie was thirteen, the Afrikaners, who are of Dutch and German origin, won control of the government. Their ancestors had settled in the southern tip of Africa in the 1650s. But the native people had been living there since ancient times.

The white settlers, soon British as well as Dutch, expanded their areas slowly at first. They were often brutal, hunting and killing the black people like animals. The blacks fought against the white invasion of their land. But by the late nineteenth century, the whites dominated almost all of what is now known as South Africa.

The discovery of great deposits of gold and diamonds around this time caused dramatic changes in South Africa. Struggles for control of the new mineral wealth and of political power led to wars between the British and Afrikaners. The British gained control of the government for half a century, then in 1948 lost out to the Afrikaners.

But the blacks had lost the right to their own land long before. The law confined them to certain parts of the country—always the poorest—except when they worked for Europeans.

Once in power, the Afrikaners cemented their racist practices into a complete system of law called *apartheid* (say it, "apart-hate"), meaning "separateness." They argued that it was God's will that South Africa should be a segregated society—with blacks kept apart from whites.

The myth of white supremacy was not new. It had been a handy tool for hundreds of years to justify the Europeans' greed for land and wealth. They spread the belief that the darker peoples were naturally inferior to the whites.

Winnie could see inequality all around her. "I became aware at an early age that the whites felt superior to us. And I could see how shabby my father looked in comparison to white teachers. That hurts your pride when you are a child." When she read about the defeat of her people, the Xhosas ("zō-sas"), in wars with the whites, she told herself, "I will start out from where those Xhosas left off and get my land back."

The anger that woke in Winnie's soul built steadily and shaped her thinking as she grew older. The songs her father brought into the classroom and their home called upon black people to unite and fight the common enemy. Winnie never forgot those songs.

Her father could not afford to buy clothes for his large family. She used to walk barefoot many miles to primary school, while the white children passed her in the buses provided only for them. She got shoes when she started going to Shawbury High School because they were part of the school uniform everyone had to wear.

At Shawbury, there was one teacher she loved very much. He couldn't say in class what he believed, or he would lose his job. But coming down the long hall to their classroom he would shout that Germany had not been unified by speeches and debates; their struggle was of "bl-o-o-o-d and iron." By the time he said "bl-o-o-o-d" he had reached the classroom. And stepping inside, he added, "And so is our struggle in this country."

"That is how I came to believe that my own struggle is to be won by blood and iron," Winnie said long after.

Her father, too, admired the Germans, but for the way they built a powerful industrial society. That was why he gave her the German name of "Winifred," which she disliked. But it soon became "Winnie." Her African name, Nomzano, means "trial" in the Xhosa language. Many harsh trials were to come in her life.

Although Winnie was a quiet young girl, her leadership was felt by the other students. The Shawbury girls elected her chief monitor. She led the debating club and won several sports trophies. An excellent student, she helped many other girls prepare for their exams. She was ready to share everything. She and her best friend used to trade dresses so no one would know they had only one school outfit each.

Winnie liked listening to debates on Africa's future by her teachers, fiercely proud of their African heritage. In her senior year, in 1952, she heard about the "Defiance Campaign." Thousands of blacks all over the country were refusing to obey the racist laws. Their leaders, including a young lawyer named Nelson Mandela, adopted Gandhi's tactic of civil disobedience. Gandhi, the leader of India, said that if you sit back and accept evil, you are as much a part of it as those who commit the evil. Africans, Indians, and a handful of whites walked into segregated "whites only" facilities to show the government they would not accept this evil.

When the people broke the law, police vans drove up quickly and hauled them off to the station, where they were often beaten or put in prison.

Winnie and her school friends lived far off in the countryside, but they learned from their teachers what was happening in the cities. They caught the word "defiance," and that was enough to spark rebellion. "Away with authority!" became their slogan at school, and Shawbury nearly closed down. But when the term ended, Winnie graduated.

Next stop? Johannesburg . . .

2

Standing Up for Everyone

It was a huge leap for Winnie, from Pondoland to Johannesburg. Not only in distance—far northwest of her birthplace—but in the kind of life she found there. Johannesburg, with more than two million people, is the biggest city in South Africa. It is in the gold-rich Transvaal region. The yellow slag heaps from the mines loom up beyond the big hotels and office buildings. In the elegant white part of the city there are homes with swimming pools and tennis courts. In the black ghettoes, the poorly paid workers live in shacks. Half of their children die before reaching the age of six.

Winnie, sixteen now, was tall and slim, with smooth skin and the beautiful face of her mother. She had come to the city to be trained as a medical social worker, a natural choice for her. She had always been interested in people, gone out of her way to help them. Now she began to learn the professional skills to do it better, and earn her living by it. In six months, she earned a scholarship that paid both tuition and boarding fees.

In Johannesburg, signs of discrimination and segregation were everywhere: EUROPEANS ONLY. WHITES ONLY. Again and again, at bus stops, movies, restaurants—even park benches. White policemen cruised the black districts in their cars, showing their guns whenever they stepped out.

The motto of Winnie's school was "Know Thyself." But finding out who you were and what you wanted from life didn't extend to taking part in politics to get what you wanted. The school would not allow that. Outside its doors, however, Winnie learned, and learned fast. For one thing, most of her neighbors belonged to labor unions and to the African National Congress. She listened to their talk, read their pamphlets, began going to their meetings. "We found ourselves talking political issues all the time," she said. Always the same names came up—Nelson Mandela, Oliver Tambo, Chief Luthuli.

Her friend Adelaide Tsukudu was in love with Oliver Tambo. She often took Winnie along when she met him. They went with other students to the huge meetings of the Congress at Trades Hall.

Winnie's table was loaded with books about politics and economics. She learned about the beginnings of the African National Congress (ANC). In the early 1900s blacks had started to organize countrywide resistance to white rule, cutting across tribal lines. They formed the ANC and gathered strength slowly. The movement spurted ahead when the Afrikaners took power in 1948 and began to build the rigid system of apartheid.

Nelson Mandela

Oliver Tambo

Chief Luthuli

Acts of nonviolent resistance, like the Defiance Campaign Winnie had been part of, increased. The government answered with new and harsher laws. In Johannesburg, for instance, certain parts of the city can be owned and occupied only by people of a particular racial group. The aim is to prevent blacks and whites living or working in the same place, and to break up the black family. A few areas are left open to all races for business or trade. Some blacks are allowed to stay in servants' quarters attached to white homes. But their husbands or wives are not allowed to live with them. Many people had to move because they were in an area meant for another race. If they refused, they went to prison.

The banning power was another weapon the Afrikaner government adopted at this time. When anyone is suspected of action against "public order," the government can issue a banning order. It bars the person from attending meetings or holding public office, from entering schools or airports or newspaper offices, from writing for publication, from being quoted in any newspaper or magazine, from leaving the district to which he or she is confined. The banned person must report regularly to the police. The ban forces a person to remain at home from 6 P.M. to 6 A.M. during the week, and from 6 P.M. Friday to 6 A.M. Monday. The banned person has no appeal to a court.

A ban order can last two or five years, and can always be renewed.

Today, the apartheid system has divided the country so that four and a half million whites, only one-sixth of the population, have control over 87 percent of the country. Blacks are allotted only 13 percent of the land, divided into ethnic "homelands." Half of the blacks live in Soweto ("So-way-toe") and similar black townships on the edges of the industrial centers, where they work but have no political rights. The blacks who live in such "white" areas are called "foreign" or "temporary" residents. Even if they were born there! They are not allowed to own land or to move about freely. All blacks over age 16 must carry a passbook—with fingerprints, a photograph, and work records—at all times.

Winnie joined in the great excitement in 1955 when a Congress of the People was called by the ANC. It met at Kliptown, just outside Johannesburg. More than 3,000 people—black, brown, white—adopted a Freedom Charter. It began: "South Africa belongs to all who live in it, black and white." After it spells out the needs of the people and the rights they claim, it ends: "These freedoms we will fight for, side by side, throughout our lives, until we have won our liberty."

When Winnie earned her diploma, she was awarded a prize as the best student. The Baragwanath Hospital in Soweto offered her a job as the first black medical social worker in South Africa. At the same time, she was given a scholarship to study sociology at an American university. It was a hard decision to make. To go abroad, see America, master a new field? Or to stay at home and help her people overcome the dreadful living conditions of Johannesburg? She chose the hospital job.

Baragwanath is still the only hospital for the million people who live in Soweto. Dr. Nthatho Motlana, who was on the staff then, remembers that even at age nineteen Winnie "worried about other people, much more than about herself." He said she was always giving needy people money out of her own pocket, little as she had.

She stood up for anyone in trouble. Once Dr. Motlana said a sick man needed to rest for three weeks. As the patient's social worker, Winnie had to tell the man's boss. He was very angry at losing the man's labor. But Winnie said firmly, "You have to accept my competence. The decision stands!" And the patient got his three weeks' sick leave.

Winnie saw Nelson Mandela for the first time in a courtroom. He was defending a friend of hers who had been arrested and beaten up by the police. "This towering, imposing man," she said, "was quite awesome."

The next time she saw him was with her friends Adelaide and Oliver Tambo. Oliver introduced her as "Winnie from Bizana." (That was Oliver's hometown too.) Soon after, Nelson invited her to lunch on a Sunday. She was very nervous. He was much older— by 18 years—and a leader everyone admired. She looked over her frilly dresses; not one of them seemed right. She borrowed something to make her seem older and more dignified.

They met at his law office, where he worked seven days a week. Files of legal papers piled high on his desk, table, chairs, the floor. He took her to an Indian restaurant. She couldn't eat the strange, spicy food, and besides, people kept coming up to their table to consult with Nelson. She felt left out.

After lunch they drove out of town to walk in the countryside. He asked if she would help raise money for the trial he and others were facing. Of course she would. As they walked back to the car, her sandal strap broke. He took her hand to help her on the rocky path. As they came to the car, he said, "It was a lovely day," and kissed her.

Nelson phoned her often; they met, talked briefly till he had to rush off to the court or a meeting. Even that early, she felt that he belonged to everyone. "Life with him was a life without him," she said. He never pretended she would have special claim to his time.

This was not a storybook romance. No time for that. Always the talk was of politics and tactics and goals.

One day, in the car, Nelson told her he knew a dressmaker she must see to have her wedding gown made. That's how it happened: no proposal. He just took for granted they would marry. All she could say was "What time?" She was madly in love with him, "and so was he with me in his own way."

Her family couldn't believe the news. Marry Nelson Mandela, their great leader? Her father was shocked. But very proud, too. Still, he worried about Nelson's future. After all, he was on trial for treason, betraying his country.

For Nelson there was never any doubt about what course to take. In his childhood he had learned from the tribal elders to love his country, and his roots. This pride in his people stood above any concern for himself.

Nelson and Winnie were married at her village home in Pondoland in June 1958.

3

So Little Time
to Love

The 22-year-old bride went to live in a little shanty in Soweto. It wasn't the kind of married life a girl dreams of, for Nelson was away most of the time. The Treason Trial—he was one of 156 accused—was going on in Pretoria, about a hundred miles north. He stayed there often to help the team of lawyers prepare the defense. When he did come home, there was hardly any time to eat or sleep. He was off to see the ANC leaders. He had been banned from holding office or attending meetings of any kind. So he had to work secretly.

Among their close friends were several women—

black, white, Indian—whom Winnie greatly admired for their faith and courage. She worked with them in the Women's Federation when it decided to organize a mass protest against the hated pass laws. If a black is found in a white area without the passbook or the proper stamp in it, it is a crime he is jailed for. A thousand blacks a day are arrested for this "crime."

Should she join in the protest? Nelson could no longer earn money. Her job at the hospital brought just enough for their food. She knew she would lose her job if she demonstrated. But without asking Nelson, she went ahead and did it. When he came home that night, she wasn't there. With thousands of other women, she had been arrested. Pregnant with her first child, she was held in prison for two weeks. She came out to find her job gone.

It was bad news, though expected. But, like Nelson, she felt "the nation came first. Everything else was second." She knew when she married him that "I married the struggle, the liberation of my people."

Prison was nothing new to her. As a social worker she visited the families of people who were in prison. These were the "forgotten people," she said, the ones whose names you never see in the news. Once, bringing food to a friend in prison, she was beaten so hard by the jailers that they broke her arm.

She decided to take classes for women who wanted

to learn to speak in public. They would write out what they had to say and then try the speech on each other. When Winnie gave her first real speech, for the Women's Federation, the audience was so excited they made up a song about her right on the spot, and sang it to her.

Two of these women, much older than Winnie, would always stand by her side. One was Helen Joseph, a white social worker. She had understood early on the need for political action to cure the social ills she saw every day. "I regard her completely as my mother," Winnie once said, "because of what she means to me not only politically, but as a human being." The other woman was Lilian Ngoyi, a black leader of both the ANC and the garment workers' union. "She made me," said Winnie; "I idolized her." Both Helen and Lilian stood accused with Nelson in the Treason Trial. Both women suffered jailing and banning.

The mounting protests against apartheid kept an international spotlight on South Africa. On March 21, 1960, a nationwide day of protest against the pass laws was called. At the black township of Sharpeville a crowd of 20,000 gathered in front of the police station. The police opened fire, killing 68 blacks and wounding 178 others. The government declared a state of emergency. The ANC was outlawed, and 12,000 people, mainly blacks, were taken in predawn

arrests. More than 5000 were convicted and sentenced to prison.

The outside world was stunned as it looked at headlines and pictures of the massacre. The "wicked myth of apartheid" was attacked in editorials and the pass laws called "an affront to humanity." South African consulates were picketed and the United Nations demanded that apartheid be abolished.

Feeling they stood alone in the world, the Afrikaners became even more stubborn about apartheid. They turned South Africa into a complete police state.

Nelson was kept in Pretoria Prison. He took over his own defense when the other lawyers resigned. One day the judge asked him whether freedom for blacks would not be a direct threat to white South Africans. He replied: "We are not antiwhite. We are against white supremacy. . . . It is quite clear that the ANC has consistently preached a policy of race harmony and we have condemned racism no matter by whom it is professed."

Winnie agreed. "We never look at people as black or white; it is the enemy who compels us to use those terms."

Nelson was let out of prison after five months, though the trial still went on. He came home to Winnie and their little girl, Zenani. A second daughter, Zindziswa, was born soon after. In March 1961 came

the verdict: not guilty. The judge ruled the state had failed to prove that the defendants called for violence.

The government gave its usual reply—sweeping arrests. Winnie hardly saw Nelson before he was gone again. The last time he was at home legally was just before he left to give his speech. He knew what would follow, but couldn't bear to tell her. He disappeared underground to continue the struggle. "I had so little time to love him," Winnie said. But that love would survive all the years of separation to come.

Not that Nelson was an angel. If they had lived a normal family life she probably would have found in him the many faults most people have. But there was only the briefest time to be with him, and the longest time to yearn for him.

She saw him often while he was underground. A knock at the window in the predawn hours signaled that he was there. But soon the police kept a 24-hour watch on her, and she had to find ways to escape them. She would be alerted to meet someone, then drive to where another car would pick her up, jump from that car into yet another; by the time she reached Nelson in one of his many hideouts, perhaps ten cars had been involved.

It was mostly whites who organized these meetings. Winnie never knew who they were. She ended up with Nelson in a white person's home, the owners gone so they could be alone together. It wasn't easy for Nelson to go unrecognized. He was a tall, striking man; the whole country knew his look. Still, he used a lot of disguises to get about.

In a letter he smuggled to the press, he told what he was doing and why: "I have had to separate myself from my dear wife and children, from my mother and sisters, to live as an outlaw in my own land. I have had to abandon my profession and live in poverty, as many of my people are doing. . . . The struggle is my life."

Winnie moved the family to a farm in Rivonia, on the outskirts of Johannesburg. Somehow Nelson was able to see them there at times. For the children it was a fleeting taste of the joy of family life. Few as these moments were, the two girls always thought of the Rivonia farm as their one true home.

Often Winnie had close shaves with the police when they put up road blocks to trap Nelson. Once, when they stopped her, she was riding in a Red Cross car with a doctor. Because her face was round and her body plump, she looked pregnant and was able to fake labor pains. The police let her through. And again:

"I remember another occasion when the old car Nelson left me gave in completely. Someone came to me that day and told me to drive to a particular corner. When I got there, a tall man in blue overalls and a chauffeur's white coat and peaked cap opened the door, ordered me to shift from the driver's seat and took over and drove. That was him. . . . He looked so different that for a moment, when he walked toward the car, I didn't recognize him myself. In broad daylight he drove to a garage and bought me a car, trading in the old one, then drove me to the center of Johannesburg. And in the thick of Sauer Street, where there are hundreds of commuters, he just stopped at a stop sign, got out, bade me good-bye and disappeared. So that was the kind of life we led."

Because they felt that Nelson was the heart of their

freedom movement, people protected him. Still, there was always the risk of an informer turning him in. To rally support abroad, he slipped out of his country and met with heads of other African states. In London he talked with political leaders, and in Algeria he took some military training. Out of his own land, for the first time in his life, he felt free. No apartheid, no hounding by the police. In other African countries he saw blacks and whites mingling peacefully.

Secretly he returned home. While he was gone, a military wing of the ANC, called Spear of the Nation, had formed to damage government property. Had not the Afrikaners answered every demand for the people's rights with brutal force? It leaves us "with only two choices: submit or fight," Nelson said. "If the government reaction is to crush by naked force our nonviolent struggle, we will have to seriously reconsider our tactics. In my mind, we are closing a chapter on this question of a nonviolent policy."

Winnie saw Nelson only once when he came back from abroad. It had to be a hurried meeting, their last private moments together for almost 25 years. Soon after, the terrible news came that Nelson had been arrested, probably on a tip from an informer. Winnie grieved, not only for herself and her children but for the struggle, for the loss of a leader. She knew it was the end of any kind of family life. But, she thought, we share this with millions of our people whose family lives have been destroyed by apartheid.

Nelson went on trial. He was sentenced to five years at hard labor. As the prison door closed on him, Winnie said, "I will continue the fight as I have always done in the past."

4

A Leader
in Her Own Right

One day in 1963 the police raided the farm in Rivonia
where Winnie was living. They captured several men
hiding nearby. That October, in Pretoria, the government put on trial 11 men—six blacks, one Indian, and
four whites. They were charged with sabotage and
plotting to overthrow the government.

In the Rivonia Trial, as it was called, Nelson was
Accused No. 1. The words he spoke in court are now
counted among the most famous defenses in history.
Yes, he had planned sabotage. But only because all
other means of opposing white supremacy were closed
by law. "We had either to accept inferiority, or fight

against it by violence." He said they chose sabotage rather than terrorism because they did not want to kill anyone. Their aim was to focus world attention on injustice in South Africa.

He spelled out what his people wanted: above all, equal political rights. The courtroom was deathly still as he came to his final words: "I have cherished the ideal of a democratic and free society in which all persons live together in harmony with equal opportunities. It is an ideal which I hope to live for and achieve. But if needs be, it is an ideal for which I am prepared to die."

He was sentenced to life imprisonment.

"Life imprisonment..." When the judge spoke those words, the crowded courtroom expected Winnie to cry. "But no," said a British reporter. "She appeared on the steps and she flashed a smile that dazzled. The effect was regal and almost triumphant, performed in the heart of the Afrikaner capital in her moment of anguish. The crowds of Africans thronging Church Square cheered...." And then, as the convicted men were taken outside to be driven off to prison, the crowd sang freedom songs and the forbidden black national anthem, "God Bless Africa."

This was the last glimpse of their father that Zindzi, now four, and Zeni, five, would have for many years.

The police would not let them get close enough to touch Nelson.

Winnie saw Nelson once more before he was sent to Robben Island, a maximum-security prison off Cape Town at the southern tip of the country. She tried to keep her pain from upsetting him. But his strength reassured her. He warned her: "You'll be blamed for what I've done. You can expect many insults. But you'll bear up under it," he said. "I know you will." And then he was gone.

The next weeks and months were terrible for her. To be all alone, to lose the husband she loved—how could she go on? She tried her best to get on with living. The police allowed Nelson to write her only once in the first six months. She read that letter over and over again as time dragged by.

Nelson was not allowed to write home about politics, only about personal matters, and then only 500 words. His letters told of the garden he had started on the prison island, of the tomato plants he was raising, of the mountains he would climb again someday. And of how much he loved and missed Winnie and Zeni and Zindzi.

Now Winnie noticed a change taking place in herself. She was no longer "just a carbon copy" of Nelson. The public had stopped saying it was "Nelson's wife" speaking. They saw she had her own voice. She was a committed fighter for black liberation.

Soon after Nelson went to prison, Winnie was placed under a banning order. The police tried to make her life miserable by hauling her into court on any excuse—or no excuse. Winnie never asked for mercy. She was not the offender; the white racists were the real criminals.

They almost always found her guilty. Except for one time when a police sergeant stamped right into her bedroom and put his hand on her shoulder to arrest her. She knocked him down so hard he broke his neck. Six men rushed in and carried her off to prison. This time, strangely, she was not declared guilty.

What hurt badly was the banning order that kept her from entering any school. "When you are a mother," she said, "the first day in school for your child is one of the greatest things. It means so much to both you and to your child. I've never been able to do that." As soon as the schools learned who the children were, they expelled them. People were too scared to have anything to do with Winnie and the girls. Winnie lost many jobs because the security police would step in and have her fired. "Divorce your husband and you can keep this job for life," one store manager told her.

The children felt insecure without a father, and with

a mother they couldn't count on to be there when they needed her. But they learned from Winnie how to live without fear. She made them strong. Once, watching her sentenced in court, Zindzi began to cry, and Winnie said, "You must never cry because you are giving them satisfaction if you do so."

One of Winnie's brothers would stay with the girls when she was away. But when she was there, she gave them all her warmth and understanding. They remember her singing them lovely Xhosa lullabies at night, playing with them, trying to be father as well as mother.

They were proud of the way she lived up to her principles. "She is a very sweet person," Zindzi said, "but when she gets into those fights with the police, it's bad; she's got a hell of a temper!"

Growing desperate, Winnie finally made the hard decision to send the children to Swaziland, a small country tucked into the northeast corner of South Africa. A white friend, Elinor Birley, took care of them and placed them in a school. She and other friends paid the fees. Here, at least, they were safe.

Meanwhile Nelson and the other Rivonia men were finding out what Robben Island was like. On its flat, bare stone sits the prison. Inside a 30-foot wall was Nelson's cell block. The prisoners worked in a lime quarry. Their food was porridge and stale vegetables. Their hard labor went on for ten years, made worse by beatings from the guards.

At first Winnie could visit Nelson only for a half hour every six months. She was not allowed to go by train or car, and the long, costly flight meant borrowing money from friends. In the visiting room, she and Nelson sat on opposite sides of a glass barrier so thick they could not see each other clearly. Unable to touch, they talked through earphones. If politics was even hinted at, the guard disconnected them. They kissed good-bye through the glass barrier.

To make life better for the prisoners, Nelson led them in hunger strikes and slowdowns. With international support, their conditions were improved. Visits and letters were increased to twice a month; hard labor was ended; newspapers were let in; they were allowed to study.

The white government, angered by a fresh outbreak of sabotage, passed a terrorism law. It gave them almost unlimited power to lock up anyone they liked without going near a court of law. Many people simply vanished. The first news of them might appear in the press: So-and-so "hanged himself," or "fell out of a window." The truth was that they died at the hands of the security police.

One midnight, Winnie's door was kicked open and

the security police came storming in. They tore her house apart looking for evidence, then dragged her off to Pretoria Prison.

She was locked up, alone, in the cell used for murderers.

5

Children Were Dying in the Street

Those first days in prison were the worst in her life. Hopeless, hopeless. Under the law, they could keep her there forever. The bleak cell, a smelly bucket for a toilet, a plastic water bottle, a mug, and the bed, a mat with filthy blankets thrown on the cement floor.

Darkness. Deathly quiet. Hours dragged by endlessly. Talking aloud to herself. Sitting, standing, pacing the few steps between the walls, lying on her back, one side, the other side . . . To fill the hours she scraped the paint off the wall with her fingernails. She spent a whole day watching two ants crawling. She ripped apart a blanket and with the threads made and remade

small ropes. Then did it with the hem of her dress. The bare bulb burning all night; sleeplessness.

Every day two women guards inspected her cell. They stripped her naked and examined every part of her clothing and body. The security police questioned her for five straight days and nights. Her body swelled with the beatings, she passed out. The police grilling her said, "You are going to be broken completely. You are a finished woman." They tried to force her to name people in the ANC, to reveal its plans. Co-operate, and we'll let you go free. You can be with your husband.

How could they think that after giving her life to this cause her principles would be for sale! But they never let up.

She was made sick by the disgusting food, her skin yellowed, her gums bled, she could not stand, she had fever and fainting spells. But she never gave in. After 491 days in prison, she and the other defendants were freed. "I got more liberated in prison," Winnie said. For blacks, "the whole country is a prison, and when you are inside, you know why you are there and the people who put you there also know."

She stepped into "freedom," only to have her ban clamped down again, this time for five years. She was under house arrest each night and weekends. Visitors were forbidden. She could not be quoted in the press.

She would live under renewed bans for almost all the years to come.

The police accused her again and again of violating the ban by having visitors. Or talking with another banned person. Or failing to report to them in Cape Town when she was visiting Nelson. Then in 1974 they sent her to another prison for six months. Her crime? Her two daughters, during a school vacation, had come from Swaziland to see her. A friend who was a banned person had taken them to meet Winnie while she was at work. The judge declared it a crime for Winnie and her friend to meet this way and "communicate."

When she came out of prison, her ban had expired. For ten months she knew a shaky "freedom." It ended after a great uprising by 20,000 students, many still in primary school, in Soweto, on the outskirts of Johannesburg. In June 1976, they marched to protest the government's order that Afrikaans must be used as the language of instruction in black schools. That was not *their* language. The deep bitterness against all the racial laws exploded when this official tongue of a hated government was forced upon them.

"I was there among them," said Winnie. "I saw what happened. The children picked up stones, they used dustbins as shields and marched towards machine guns. Children were dying in the street, and as they were dying, the others marched forward, facing guns. This is what happens when you hunger for freedom. Nothing else matters."

That terrible week Winnie organized a Black Parents Association (BPA), to support the children. "If we let them down now," she said, "they will spit on our graves one day." She was the only woman, and her leadership helped bridge the gap between young and old. They raised money to bury the dead, they fed families, they cared for orphans, they pleaded with the police to stop firing on children.

Dr. Motlana said Winnie was "powerful, faithful, honest. And above all, brave." When a police commander accused her of having started the uprising, she yelled at him, "You bloody murderer, killing our children, and you tell us *we* started the riots!" She was scared of nothing and nobody.

Riots erupted all over Soweto as the army joined the police to put down the rebellion. The death toll mounted daily for a week. Most of the victims were under age 18.

Winnie was among the thousands arrested. The police kept her in prison for four months. A woman jailed with her said Winnie never let up on the officials. She demanded better conditions and got the women to back her. "She was forever ready to listen, to smile, to comfort. And if you needed help, to act.

She was motherly; to the young, to the old, she was the same."

In prison, Winnie was visited by her daughter Zeni. It was the same prison Winnie had been in 18 years before, when she was pregnant with Zeni. Change? Progress? After all those years of struggle for the same ideals? The loving letters between her and Nelson crossing cold stone walls kept their spirits from being shattered.

Zindzi, who had now turned 16, was allowed to visit her father for the first time. Strange, to be introduced to your father at this age, and inside a prison. She was very nervous, but Nelson was warm and loving and so proud of her that she lost her fear.

After Soweto, many students fled the police to study abroad or get military training. Others were jailed on Robben Island, where Nelson helped them continue their studies. The island soon came to be called Mandela University.

Then, one night in 1977, at four A.M., Winnie and Zindzi woke to heavy knocking and loud barking at the door. Winnie opened the door to find men with guns and dogs outside. They were being forced to leave their home in Soweto. The men grabbed everything in the house, tossed it into an army truck, and drove them about 300 miles south to a black township outside Brandfort. They dumped her in a tiny house kneedeep in rubbish. No electricity, no running water, no stove, no bath, one mattress on the dirt floor. For Zindzi it was a fierce shock, and for Winnie, heartache that her commitment should bring this upon her own daughter.

She found her new neighbors had been warned to keep away from her on pain of arrest. But blacks had found out long ago that if the white government says someone is bad, she must be very good. They all knew about Nelson Mandela. Now here was his wife, a woman with a warm, welcoming smile, large dark eyes that showed her feelings—pain, sorrow, and yet humor too. She wore a long African dress, with a scarf around her head in the Xhosa style. Her voice was clear and melodious. Straight, beautiful, she carried herself like an African queen. During the day they dared not speak to her. But at night they left small parcels of food—some beans or cabbage—at her door.

The Orange Free State, as this area is called, is the heartland of the Afrikaners. Yet Winnie dared enter the shops no black went into. At the police station and the post office she used the white entrance. At the supermarket, blacks bought from outside through a small window. But Winnie stalked into the front door and enjoyed seeing the white shoppers run out till she had finished her shopping.

She found the Brandfort ghetto to be near star-

vation. Droughts had ruined white farmers. They sold their land, putting blacks out of work and out of home. The blacks ended up being taken to "homelands" they had never heard of. Or they broke the law and hid in Brandfort's ghetto. Nine thousand people going hungry, sickening, their babies dying.

Winnie opened a nursery in a church and trained women to help. The children lived on farms outside the town, and had to get up in the dark to walk about five miles to school on empty stomachs. After school, Winnie fed them their one hot meal, from a huge pot of soup she kept on the stove. Then they walked all the way back home. Winnie's house became a clinic and welfare station, aided by the charity of friends. She learned Sotho, the local language.

Winnie's example led to many changes in Brandfort. The blacks stopped working on farms or in shops for only fifty cents a day. They refused to buy in stores that would not let them try on clothing. They refused to shop through "those silly little windows."

What is normal anywhere else, Winnie thought, we must fight for in South Africa.

6

The Future Lies
in Black Hands

And so she has fought, year after year. Almost daily she was seized in Brandfort for breaking the ban orders. Many charges were brought against her, but what is the difference, she thought—being banned or unbanned? In prison or not? Every black person is in prison in South Africa; it is only the size of the prison that differs.

In 1982 Nelson was moved from Robben Island to Pollsmoor Prison on the mainland near Cape Town. Here conditions were worse. But Winnie was heartened by a "Free Mandela" campaign that won worldwide support. The American and British governments joined in urging his release. Nelson had become the symbol of all political prisoners in South Africa.

A wave of fresh rebellion in 1983 saw the freedom movement reborn. The new United Democratic Front (UDF), said Winnie, "is our South Africa of tomorrow." The UDF spoke for two million South Africans of all races. At its founding meeting, 12,000 people cheered at the reading of a defiant message from Nelson, smuggled out of prison.

Winnie knew what made this hopeful change possible. Huge numbers of black people had recently come into the cities where the jobs were. And a new generation of primary and high school students had turned politically active. Moving together, they carried out an open declaration of war against apartheid.

The pace of protest speeded up. In July 1985, the government imposed a state of emergency on many black districts. It sent in waves of police.

Then a gasoline bomb wrecked Winnie's home in Brandfort. With her life in danger from government terrorists, she went back to her house in Soweto. At gunpoint, the police ordered her to leave. When she refused, they dragged her off to court. As she came out, crowds surrounded her and chanted ANC slogans. Back to Soweto she went.

Bombs and land mines began exploding in white shopping malls and vacation resorts, killing and injuring some whites. The Black Sash, a white women's legal-aid group, warned that apartheid was driving the country into civil war.

Winnie broke her ban again to speak at a public funeral of black children shot by the police: "As we have had to bury our children today, so shall the blood of these heroes be avenged. The future of the country lies in black hands."

When she defied the ban on public speaking yet again, the police arrested her, then released her on bail. They plainly feared that putting another Mandela in prison would be too dangerous.

But they went on trying to scare her. On the way into Soweto the police forced her car off the road, then banged her two-year-old grandchild's head against the car door. She shoved them away. She had had enough of going along with these bans, she said. "What I stand for is what they want to banish. I couldn't think of a greater honor."

Inside South Africa no one could hear her voice. No newspaper, radio, or television station could carry her message. But her words raced around the globe.

Help us, she called, you who believe that all people are created equal. Stop sending arms and technology to South Africa. Refuse to trade with this

country while it remains in chains. Ask your government to condemn racism here just as you condemn
it at home. Are you for good or evil? For justice or
injustice?

Who did not know the answer?

ABOUT THIS BOOK

It was in the fall of 1985 that I began to see Winnie Mandela's name in my morning paper almost every day. At night, on the TV news, there she was again, protesting injustice, demanding equality. In the streets of South Africa I saw her people clubbed by police, shot by police, jailed by police.

For what? For wanting everything Americans believe in. For everything the Reverend Martin Luther King, Jr., cried out for in the long civil-rights struggle that broke the barriers of racism in America.

Winnie Mandela's fight for freedom is ours, too. If racism prevails anywhere, freedom is threatened everywhere. So I went to work to learn all I could about her story. Most helpful was the book of interviews with Winnie, her family, and her friends: *Part of My Soul Went with Him.* I used many other books and articles about South Africa.

I regret that I could not talk with Winnie Mandela, so far away and banned from speaking to writers. But I hope this book gives the reader some sense of what this magnificent woman is like, and of the passion for freedom in the soul of her people.   **M.M.**